THE STEP BY STEP ART OF
Nature Crafts

Published by
CHARTWELL BOOKS, INC.
A Division of **BOOK SALES, INC.**
110 Enterprise Avenue
Secaucus, New Jersey 07094

CLB 3310
© 1994 CLB Publishing, Godalming, Surrey, England
Printed and bound in Singapore by Tien Wah Press
All rights reserved
ISBN 0-7858-0069-7

THE STEP BY STEP ART OF

Nature Crafts

PAMELA WESTLAND

Photography by
NELSON HARGREAVES

CHARTWELL
BOOKS, INC.

Contents

Materials

Nature crafts can be as wide-ranging as you want them to be - pretty as a twist of ivy and wild roses ringing a party table, or exuberant as a cluster of hogweed stems arranged with a bright palette of garden flowers. These crafts can also be as instantly pleasing or as time-consuming as you wish - quick, easy and effective when sticking a handful of shells to a favourite straw hat, for example, or more absorbing when covering a polystyrene shape with a patchwork of leaves you have pressed.

The natural resources for the crafts shown throughout the book are to be found wherever you live, and wherever you happen to be. And to help you think laterally, and to find inspiration in a diversity of environments, the craft projects are grouped by location, the designs created with materials you can find in woodland, on the seashore, by the wayside, in the garden and market.

Woodland

A walk through a wood is a fascinating treasure hunt once you become nature-craft aware. Look for fallen twigs with interesting shapes; for small branches covered with cones or lichen; for small hollow logs that would make rugged containers for woody flower arrangements; and for clumps of wind-dried moss. Pick up fallen seedcases beneath horse chestnut and beech trees, the winged seedpods of sycamore and maple and any glistening brown nuts concealed among the fallen leaves.

Look closely at those leaves and pick up a handful in all shapes, sizes and colours, but be selective. Insect-damaged leaves rarely look attractive. Deep-cut maple leaves can be gilded to add a glint and glister to essentially brown decorations; others can be pressed for later use in wreaths and as parcel trims. Take a large bag or basket and fill it with pine, larch or other cones, contrasting them on site for size, shape and colour.

▲ *Woodland treasure* ▼ *Decorative beachcombings* ▼ *Wonders of the wayside*

Seashore

Walking on the beach is synonymous with beachcombing when there are so many seashore designs to create. Look for small pieces of weathered and bleached driftwood to give structure to flower arrangements or just to hang on the wall. Pick up obviously discarded pieces of rope - the more frayed, salt- and sun-bleached the better - to make authentic hangings for wreaths and other wall decorations. Gather up clumps of dried seaweed, the foliage of the seashore, that contrasts so well with craggy and pearly shells.

As for collecting shells, that is a pastime in its own right. There is a variety of ways you can display shells - in a jar; on a wreath, basket or jug; on parcels; as a piece of sculpture; and many more. Take a large basket with you.

Wayside

Fields, meadows, hedgerows and waysides are rich with materials that are there for the taking, and with others that are not. Before you cut or gather any wild materials, be sure that you know the current regulations pertaining to that area; they vary from country to country, and state to state. It is normally an offence to pick any wild flowers except those classified, locally, as rampant weeds, and to dig up any wild plants unless you have permission of the landowner.

On the plus side, that leaves trails of ivy to wind around napkins, glasses and candlesticks; clumps of wheat, oats, linseed and barley gathered close to agricultural land; feathery, decorative grasses, and vibrant flowers that contrast as well with them in the home as they do in the wild.

Country Garden

If you have access to a prolific garden, you have the natural resources to compose colourful wreaths and elegant table centre designs, romantic posies and nostalgic basket arrangements, and not all on a summer's day. Autumn vegetables such as gourds and corncobs, and less seasonal pickings such as cauliflower and broccoli, all have a place in the nature-craft treasury.

▲ *Country garden* ▼ *Exotic market produce*

Market Stall

Not many of us can grow sharp-coloured citrus fruits, exotic watermelons, and vibrant peppers and chillies, but to those with an eye for design the produce available in the market has a part to play in making decorations. Contrast these high-profile colours and textures with the soft earthy-browns of fragrant spices, including cinnamon sticks and nutmegs. Gather fallen rose petals and pretty flowers, select snippings from your dried flower collection and bring them together attractively and aromatically in pot pourris of all kinds. These same fragrant, earthy-brown spices become the hidden ingredients that turn everyday plant materials into delightful environmental perfumes.

Equipment

Many nature craft designs have their roots deeply planted in tradition. They date from the days when it was the custom for people, from young children to farmworkers, to sit in the fields weaving and plaiting stems into decorative and symbolic shapes, without the aid of any tools or equipment. Festival wreaths and garlands are examples of this age-old country craft. Other designs and arrangements, and this includes many wreath styles, are easier to compose with the aid of pre-formed shapes, stem-holding materials, wires and tapes, collectively known as mechanics; and almost every design is better constructed for the use of sharp, efficient scissors and secateurs. The illustrations on these pages show the materials that will, over time, make designing with natural materials a simpler and more pleasing craft.

Wreath Bases

Some wreath bases are so attractive that they may be displayed with only minimal decoration, perhaps a cluster of cones or a flamboyant bow. These include bases made of intertwined willow or vine stems; those made of ornamental grass or other dried seedheads; of cut dried grasses, and of plaited straw, woven in the manner of corn dollies.

Any of these wreath forms can be used to make up a lasting decoration using dried plant materials from air-dried garden flowers to gourds, cones and clusters of spices. For short-term display these natural stem bases may also be decorated with fresh flowers and fruits.

Dry foam ring forms, which are usually grey with a sparkly appearance, are purpose-made for use with dried flowers. Absorbent foam rings, pre-formed with a waterproof base, are specifically for use with fresh flowers. When soaked they offer the plant materials a moisture source and give a fresh-flower design a longer shelf-life.

▲ A wealth of wreath bases

Containers

It is scarcely surprising that the word 'vase' has almost slipped from popular usage. When it comes to selecting a container to display plant materials as diverse as arching twigs and delicate primroses, exotic strelitzias and clumps of seaweed, even a hollowed log or an empty seedcase may be suitable.

Some of the most pleasing partnerships of container and plant materials are achieved when there is a textural contrast between the two. Dried flowers and leaves look particularly effective in glistening glass, a pearly shell or a polished willow basket, and high-gloss materials like peppers, chillies and strawberries, are seen to best advantage against a more muted background.

Holding Materials

The use of stem-holding materials makes composing a design much easier, and makes possible styles and shapes that would not otherwise be achieved. Place a cluster of stems in a narrow-necked jug and they will remain more or less vertical; place them in a

▲ A diversity of containers

wide-necked container and they will separate to form a fan shape; but fill the neck of the container with stem-holding foam and the stems may be placed horizontally or to slant steeply downwards.

Both dry and absorbent stem-holding foam is sold in blocks which may be cut to any size and shape, in cylinders, spheres and cones, and in wreath shapes. Absorbent foam should be soaked in cold water for about 20 minutes, until it is thoroughly saturated, and should then be kept constantly moist. To re-use soaked foam, store it in a sealed plastic bag. Once it has dried out it will not reabsorb water.

To locate the foam in a wide or shallow container you may use a plastic prong secured with a strip of florists' adhesive clay (see pages 18-19). To secure foam firmly in a container, and to fix a container to a pedestal or other stand, you can use strips of florists' adhesive tape which is sold in a variety of colours.

Florists' extra-hard clay or standard modelling clay (Plasticine) may be used to secure a branch or a cluster of tall stems in a pot. When the design has extra weight at the top a heavy metal pinholder, anchored with adhesive clay, gives extra security.

Wire mesh netting, especially if it is plastic-coated, offers an alternative method of holding stems. Crumple it into a ball, push it into the neck of a container and secure it with florists' adhesive tape (see pages 18-19).

Wiring and Cutting

Good cutting equipment is essential if plants or stems are not to be damaged. Use secateurs for the thickest materials, and florists' scissors for all other stems. These should never be used to cut wire. To cut stub wires, roll wire and other types you should use purpose-made wirecutters.

Use stub wires, which are sold in packets in a variety of thicknesses and lengths, to mount flowers, cones and shells onto false stems and onto wreath bases or other decorative forms.

Use fine silver roll wire, which resembles fuse wire, to bind the stems of posies, and to bind foliage and flowers to a garland core, which may be rope, string or coiled paper. Green garden twine and raffia may also be used in these ways.

▼ *A variety of stem-holding materials* ▲ *Wiring and cutting equipment* ▼ *Decorative materials*

Bind false wire stems with gutta-percha tape, which is self-adhesive, to make them look more natural in arrangements and bouquets.

Glue can take the place of wires in fixing plant materials to a wreath base or garland, and a hot glue gun is especially useful.

Decorative Materials

Ribbons and candles can provide the finishing touch to nature crafts of all kinds - try ribbon bows on an indoor table-top, trailing ribbons on a floral 'torch' decoration and aromatic beeswax candles in an ivy-clad candleholder. Rolled beeswax candles have a special affinity with natural materials with the bonus of a subtle, indigenous aroma.

A candle spike, a plastic holder with a sharp pointed spike, is useful to fix dinner candles (with 2.5 cm/1 in diameter) into a foam ring. It avoids splitting and breaking the foam.

Techniques

Wiring Techniques

Knowing how to wire flowers, cones, shells and other materials greatly increases the range of designs you can create. Flowers that have been dried on very short stems or those like strawflowers which easily become separated from their natural stems can be mounted onto wires which are then bound with florists' tape in a neutral colour.

Pine, larch and many other cones may be secured on wires and then, on their false stems, attached to a wreath base or garland core, or inserted into stem-holding foam in a floral arrangement. Shells may be wired in a similar way for a variety of decorative uses.

Many designs, including both wreaths and garlands, are most easily composed of flowers and foliage, seedheads and grasses formed first into small posies or bunches. Use fine silver roll wire, green or brown binding twine - garden twine - or raffia to bind the stems according to the style of the finished piece.

1 *This technique may be used for all those flowers, fresh or dried, which have a deep calyx, such as carnations and pinks. Use fine-gauge stub wires for fresh flowers that are to be arranged in a bridal bouquet or headdress, and medium or thick-gauge stub wires to create false stems on those which are to be used in a floral arrangement. Push one end of the stub wire horizontally through the calyx and bend down the short end of the wire.*

2 *Twist together the two pieces of wire just below the calyx until the end of the short piece protrudes as little as possible from the long wire 'stem'.*

3 *Cover the wire with gutta-percha tape, also called florists' tape, which is available in green, brown and cream. Wrap one end of the tape around the wire at the base of the calyx. Then twist the flower so that the tape, which is self-adhesive, wraps around the wire, overlapping all the way down. When the tape reaches the end of the wire, twist the tape tightly and cut off the free end.*

4 *To wire a composite flower such as a strawflower, push a medium-gauge stub wire from the back up through the centre of the flower. Bend a small hook in the wire and gently pull the wire downwards, so that the hook is concealed within the flower centre.*

5 *Use a medium-gauge stub wire to create a false stem on a cone. Wrap one end of the wire tightly around the lowest layer of 'petals' and bend the wire down beneath the cone.*

6 *Twist the two ends of the wire tightly together beneath the cone. If the false stem is likely to be seen in a design, as it may be in a floral arrangement, cover the wire with gutta-percha tape.*

7 *Study the line and form of each shell carefully before deciding how to wire it. You may use fine silver wire or medium-gauge stub wires, depending on the style of the ultimate arrangement. If the shell has a small hole, simply thread a wire through that and twist the two ends to secure them. If not, wrap a wire tightly around the centre of the shell and twist the ends together. This is easier to do with species such as nutmeg shells and mitre shells, which are ridged. Those with a smooth surface, such as marginellas, may need a dab of glue between the shell and the wire to prevent slipping.*

8 *To bind a posy of dried materials, arrange the stems loosely in one hand so that the flowers and seedheads are not cramped. Cut the stems to an even length, and wrap one end of the wire tightly around them, just below the flower heads. (It is best to use fine silver wire if the heads of one posy will overlap and conceal the stems of the next.) Bind the wire three or four times around the stems, until they are held securely, and then cut off the wire. Neaten the stem ends if necessary.*

If you wish to use twine as stem binding, leave a short end and tie the two ends together once the stems are held in place.

9 *Arrange and bind posies of fresh flowers and foliage in a similar way. Take care not to pull the binding material too tightly; this might crush the stems, and prevent them from taking up moisture. If fresh posies are to be arranged on a wreath or garland, bridal headdress or special occasion hat, leave them in water for as long as possible before arranging.*

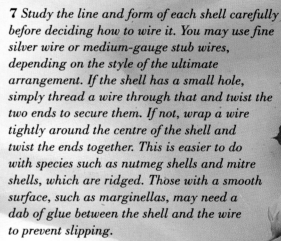

Making Wreaths and Garlands

Wreaths and garlands are among the most decorative of ways to display natural materials, from posies of fresh or dried flowers to bunches of vegetables, from gold-sprayed gourds to cinnamon sticks.

In many cases the wreath form or garland core you use will be attractive enough to be left partially on view, as when a raffia-covered ring forms part of the design or an area of intertwined vine stems is only partially covered with the decorative materials. In other cases, and particularly when a wreath is based on dry or absorbent stem-holding foam, this core material must be completely concealed. A light covering of dry hay or sphagnum moss introduces a natural element, as when it is used to cover the inner core - it may be rope, cord or string - of a garland.

The photographs show you the basic cover-up techniques, and how to make a wreath from widely contrasting materials.

1 *This type of wreath base, made of twisted vine twigs, is widely available in florists' shops. You can choose whether you cover it completely, or leave part of the base visible.*

To cover it with posies of fresh or dried flowers, cut medium-gauge stub wires in half and bend them over to make U-shaped staples. Hold the posy stems flat against the base, at any angle the design requires, and press the bent wire over them and into the wreath base. Bend back the wire ends to secure them at the side or reverse of the stem wreath.

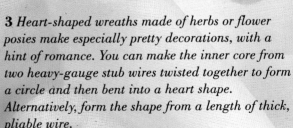

2 *Covering a dry foam ring with dry hay or moss transforms it from a purely utilitarian item into a decorative one. Press small handfuls of hay or moss against the top and sides of the foam and hold them in place with a U-shaped staple made from a length of stub wire.*

3 *Heart-shaped wreaths made of herbs or flower posies make especially pretty decorations, with a hint of romance. You can make the inner core from two heavy-gauge stub wires twisted together to form a circle and then bent into a heart shape. Alternatively, form the shape from a length of thick, pliable wire.*

If you wish to decorate the heart with small sprays of flowers and foliage, perhaps for a bridal decoration, bind the wire with white gutta-percha tape or satin ribbon.

If you intend to cover it with, for example, wired cones or dried flower posies, you can conceal the wire by covering it with dry hay or moss.

4 *A double wire ring frame, which is available in both a flat or slightly 'dished' form, can be decorated with fresh or dried flowers, woodland finds such as cones, seedcases and feathers, or fresh and dried vegetables.*

Covering the frame with dry hay or sphagnum moss conceals the wire and gives the base more 'body'. Tie a length of twine firmly to the wire and use it to bind on handfuls of dry hay or moss. Tie the twine to secure it when the ring is completely covered.

5 *If you are using rope, cord or twine as the inner core of a garland you may wish to give it more substance, and a more natural look, by covering it with dry hay or sphagnum moss. To do this, tie binding twine to one end of the rope. Wrap small handfuls of the covering material round the rope and bind them on with twine. Tie the twine securely at the other end of the rope.*

There may be other occasions when, for example, you have chosen a colour co-ordinated cord or length of unfurled paper ribbon; here, short lengths of the exposed material can form a decorative feature of the design.

6 *You can make a wreath or garland core from natural stems such as grass or wild carrot. Cut the stems when they are moist and supple and cut off most of the seedheads; a few are decorative. Gather the stems into bunches of eight to ten, secure the twine at one end and bind along the length of the stems. Join in more stems as necessary.*

7 *To form the stems into a circle, bind the two ends securely together and tie the twine to fasten it. Shape the stems into a round by easing them gently with both hands.*

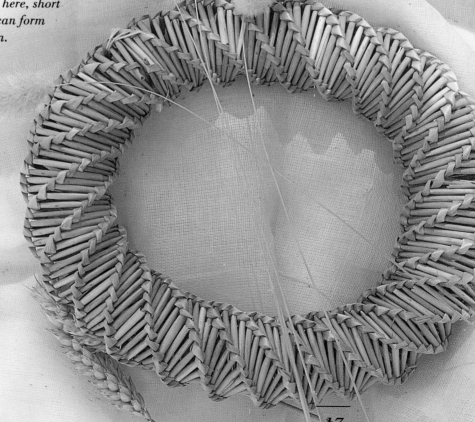

Preparing Containers

The preparation of containers from baskets to beakers, cups to candlesticks, plays a determining role in the ultimate design you can achieve. If, for example, you use a deep container with a relatively narrow opening the stems you arrange will stay more or less upright, whereas those arranged in a vessel with a wider neck will fan out all around or may even topple over the sides.

By using any one of a number of stem-holding materials you can control the angle at which the stems are held, and therefore the shape and form of the arrangement. More details of the types of 'mechanics' available are on pages 12 and 13.

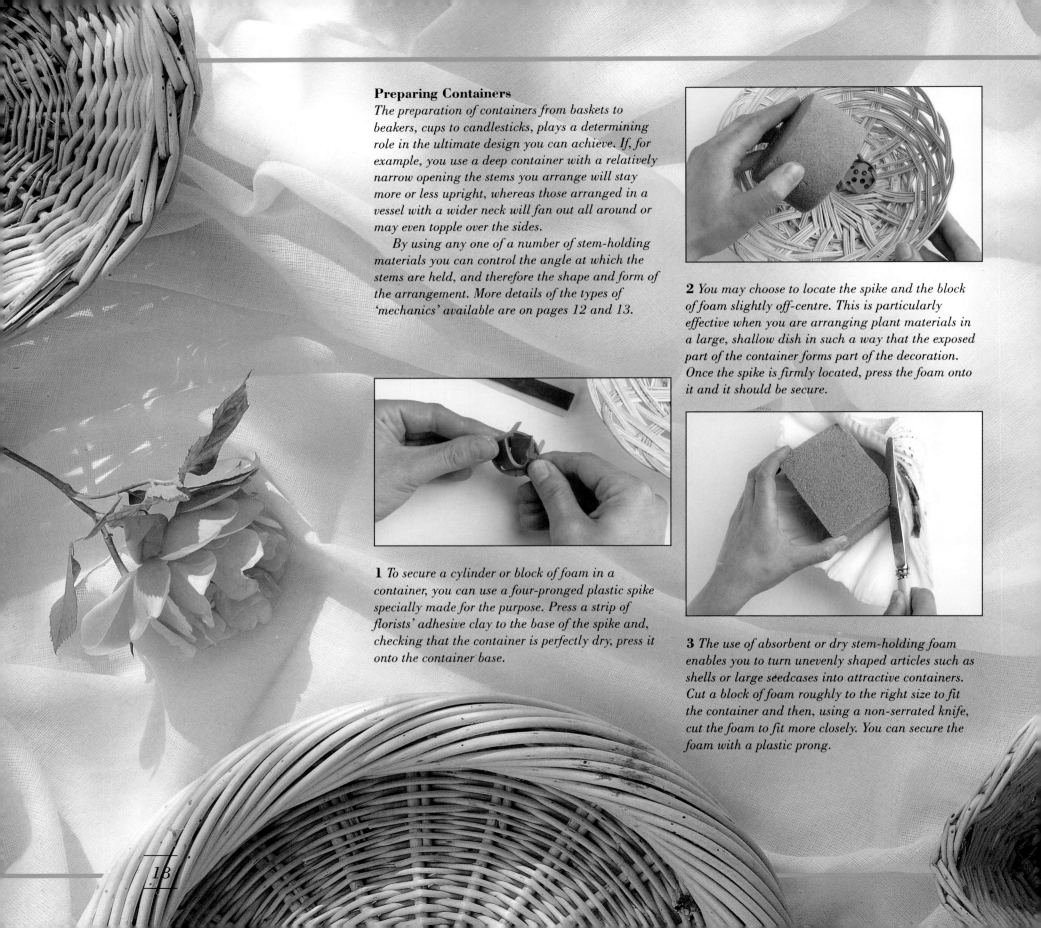

2 You may choose to locate the spike and the block of foam slightly off-centre. This is particularly effective when you are arranging plant materials in a large, shallow dish in such a way that the exposed part of the container forms part of the decoration. Once the spike is firmly located, press the foam onto it and it should be secure.

1 To secure a cylinder or block of foam in a container, you can use a four-pronged plastic spike specially made for the purpose. Press a strip of florists' adhesive clay to the base of the spike and, checking that the container is perfectly dry, press it onto the container base.

3 The use of absorbent or dry stem-holding foam enables you to turn unevenly shaped articles such as shells or large seedcases into attractive containers. Cut a block of foam roughly to the right size to fit the container and then, using a non-serrated knife, cut the foam to fit more closely. You can secure the foam with a plastic prong.

4 *Tall articles such as candlesticks, carafes, wine bottles and decorative perfume or cosmetic bottles can be used as pedestals to compose an off-the-table arrangement. To achieve graceful, flowing lines which look well in a design of this type, use a cylinder of stem-holding foam so that some stems may be angled horizontally and others trail over the rim.*

Use a purpose-made plastic 'candle cup', which has a small 'plug' on the base, or a standard plastic foam-holding saucer. Each has an indent just the right size to hold a foam cylinder. Cut strips of florists' adhesive clay and stick them to the underside of the plastic holder, making sure that they are positioned so that they will come into contact with the pedestal. Press the holder to the top of the pedestal. To complete the preparation, press the foam cylinder into the plastic holder.

5 *Crumpled wire mesh netting creates a network of criss-crossed wires with small holes between them. This method of stem-holding is suitable for use in jugs, mugs, beakers and upright vases and in wider-necked containers such as preserving pans and shopping baskets.*

When fresh flowers are arranged, the angles at which you may position the stems are limited by the plants' need to reach the water. With dry materials the wire netting may extend above the container rim so that stems may be positioned horizontally and sloping downwards.

Cut a piece of 5 cm (2 in) wire mesh netting - the plastic-covered type is easier to use - and, using both hands, crumple it into a ball. Push the netting into the neck of the container, and shape it in a mound extending 2.5-5 cm (1-2 in) above the rim, depending on the scale of the design.

6 *Tuck in any rough edges of the wire. Cut short lengths of florists' adhesive tape and loop each one around the wire, close to the container rim. Press both ends of the tape onto the container as close to the rim as possible.*

When completing the arrangement, check that the lowest leaves or other materials conceal the holding tape.

Making Bows

Full, flouncy ribbon bows provide the perfect finishing touch to decorations of all kinds, from wreaths and garlands to floral arrangements and gift parcels. You can choose ribbons to harmonize with the colours forming the design, or create an eye-catching focal point with contrasting shades. You may decide to make simple two-loop bows or, using the same technique, double up on the colour and effect by using two shades of ribbon together. Developing the technique one stage further, you can make bows with four or more loops just by twisting in one length of ribbon after another.

The step-by-step photographs show how easily you can achieve bows with a professional look.

2 *Pinch the ribbon lengths together at the centre and bind with fine silver wire or a fine-gauge stub wire. Cut the ends of the ribbon slantwise and ease out the loops so that they conceal the wire.*

1 *Paper ribbon is often tightly coiled. Carefully pull the ribbon on both sides to start unravelling the end, and then pull it apart gently all along the length. To make a two-loop bow, fold the ribbon to make a figure of eight shape, holding it together at the centre.*

3 *To make a two-loop bow with two coloured ribbons, place the ribbons one on top of the other. Form them into a figure of eight shape and bind the centre with wire.*

4 *Neaten the ends of the ribbon by cutting them slantwise. When the bow is formed of two contrasting colours it is effective to cut the upper ribbon slightly shorter than the other.*

5 *To make a false loop on a bow, cut a short length of paper ribbon and fold it to make a narrow strip - the actual size will depend on the size of the bow. Wrap the strip round the centre of the bow and glue or pin the ends to secure them at the back.*

6 *To make a four-loop bow, form the first two loops into a figure of eight. Holding the ribbon firmly in the centre, form another loop from the long end of the ribbon and hold this in place.*

7 *Form another bow from the long end of the ribbon and hold the design firmly in the centre. You can go on adding more loops in this way to make a multi-looped bow. To finish the bow, bind the centre with wire and ease the loops to cover it.*

Woodland

A walk in the woods can reward you with twigs and branches, nuts and cones, moss and leaves, seedcases and feathers - a treasure trove of decorative materials to compose long-lasting designs.

Woodland

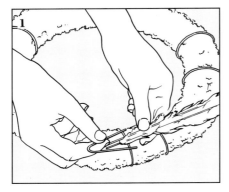

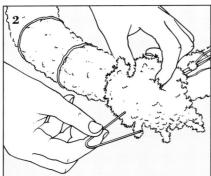

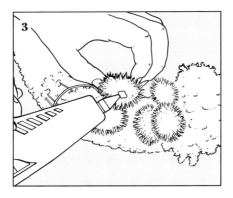

You will need:
Selection of dried materials such
as twigs, feathers, cones,
mushrooms, chestnuts, horse
chestnuts and their seedcases,
sprays of leaves, lichen, moss
A stem ring
25 cm (10 in) in diameter
Florists' scissors
Medium-gauge stub wires
Hot glue or
clear quick-setting glue
Wirecutters
Silver roll wire

1 Cut stub wires in half and bend
them to make U-shaped staples.
Attach clusters of twigs slantwise
to the ring base.

2 Take clumps of lichen and
moss and attach them at intervals
around the ring with the wire
staples.

3 Glue horse chestnut cases in
clusters, one on top of the other,
to create height and areas of
strong texture.

▶ Take a basket with you on a
woodland walk and you can
collect seedcases, cones, leaves,
twigs, moss and feathers to make
a decorative ring with subtle
contrast of both textures and
colours. A section of the
woodland ring in close up (page
25) shows the variety of textures
of these natural materials.

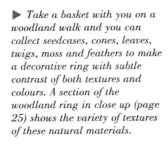

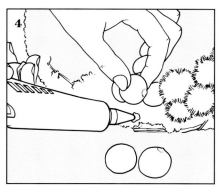

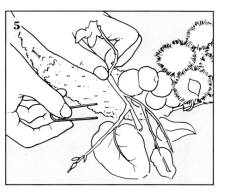

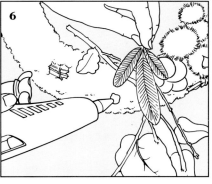

▲ *Pine cones glued together to form a single or double ring make attractive holders for scented or beeswax candles.*

4 Glue chestnuts or horse chestnuts in clusters. Hold each one in position for a few seconds to allow the glue to set.

5 Use wire staples to attach small, dense sprays of dried leaves to extend beyond the ring.

6 Use silver wire to bind clusters of four or five pheasants' feathers together, then glue them to the ring.

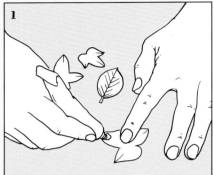

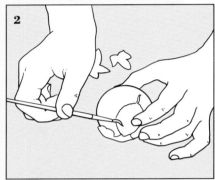

You will need:
Selection of pressed leaves
in a variety of shapes,
sizes and colours
A styrofoam ball 7.5-10.5 cm
(3-4½ in) in diameter
Clear papercraft glue
A small paintbrush

1 *Spread glue evenly over the reverse side of each leaf. Press each one onto the ball, overlapping the leaves so that the foam is completely covered.*

2 *Use a small paintbrush to brush off any powdered fall-out from the styrofoam, and to press the leaves in place.*

▲ Small parcels wrapped in plain or textured papers have a look of individuality when they are tied around with leather thonging, raffia or string, and decorated with one, two or three pressed leaves.

◄ A patchwork of fallen leaves glued to a styrofoam ball makes an unusual decoration that can be displayed in a variety of ways.

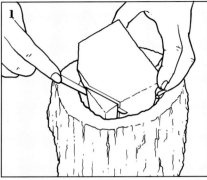

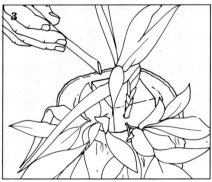

You will need:
Strelitzias
Large poppies
Peony or other large leaves
Florists' scissors
A hollow log about
30 cm (12 in) high
Absorbent stem-holding foam
A knife

▲ *A handful of dainty spring flowers, including primroses and bluebells, contrast effectively with the container, a large coconut-like seedpod, available from some florists. The seedcase is first fitted with a small, water-holding container.*

1 *Cut the block of foam to fit tightly in the hollow. Soak the foam in water.*

2 *Arrange short sprays of foliage to cover the foam and form a 'forest floor' foundation.*

3 *Cut the strelitzias at a sharp angle so that they can readily absorb moisture. Arrange the stems evenly around the container. Position the poppies so that the flower heads are below the strelitzias.*

Woodland

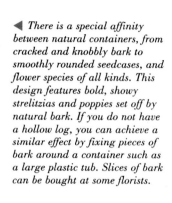

◄ *There is a special affinity between natural containers, from cracked and knobbly bark to smoothly rounded seedcases, and flower species of all kinds. This design features bold, showy strelitzias and poppies set off by natural bark. If you do not have a hollow log, you can achieve a similar effect by fixing pieces of bark around a container such as a large plastic tub. Slices of bark can be bought at some florists.*

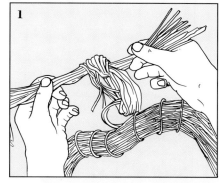

You will need:
Pine and larch cones
A heart-shaped twig
wreath 25 cm (10 in) across
Raffia
Scissors
Hot glue or
clear quick-setting glue

▲ *Split seedcases of flor de Madeira, which you can buy at some florists, make pretty heart-shaped containers for pot pourri or a mixture of dried spices.*

1 Gather raffia strands to make a thick bundle and tie them around a loop on the wreath. Twist a loop in the raffia half-way up and tie the ends in a knot.

2 Select pine cones of even size and glue them close together around the face of the wreath. Glue a larger one above the others, in the centre. Grade the larch cones for size and shape, and glue them together inside the ring of pine cones.

◄ *Choose cones of differing size, shape and colour to create an effective two-tone wreath with the appearance of an intricate wood carving.*

31

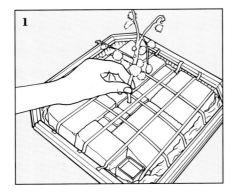

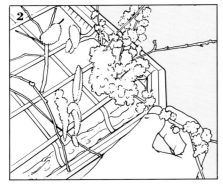

1 *Line the basket with a piece of polyethylene. Cut blocks of absorbent foam to fit, soak them in water and place them in the basket with the small container. Stick strips of adhesive tape from side to side of the basket. Position twigs of pussy willow just off-centre of the basket, arranging them to branch off in opposing directions.*

2 *Cut short twigs with clusters of catkins and position them close to the taller pussy willow ones. Create a patch of hawthorn blossom at one corner of the basket, positioning the stems to face in varying directions.*

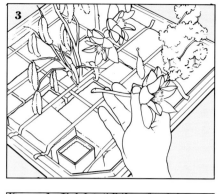

◄ *Twigs, blossom, flowers and foliage are arranged in a foam-filled basket to create an indoor garden reminiscent of a forest in springtime. Make sure you do not pick flowers such as bluebells or primroses in the wild – you can grow them in the garden, or even in pots and troughs on a windowsill.*

You will need:
Pussy willow twigs, hawthorn blossom, and any twigs with catkins
Flowers such as bluebells or grape hyacinth, primrose or primula, narcissi and lesser celandine
Trails of ivy leaves
Dried moss
A shallow basket about 30 cm (12 in) square
A piece of polyethylene liner
Absorbent stem-holding foam
A knife
Florists' adhesive tape
Small water-holding container
A skewer

3 *Cut short the narcissi stems and position them so that the flowers form patches of 'ground cover' beneath the twigs. If the narcissi stems are weak, pierce holes in the foam before positioning them.*

4 *Arrange a cluster of the small primula flowers in the container of water. Pierce holes at the other side of the basket and arrange the celandines. Cover visible areas of the foam with clumps of moss, to represent the forest floor.*

▲ *This hollowed-out seedpod, available from a florists, looks rather like a large fir cone. Filled with absorbent foam, it makes a pretty container for a selection of delicate flowers.*

Woodland

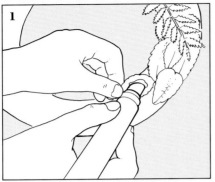

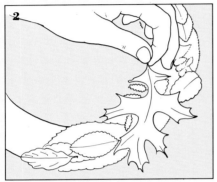

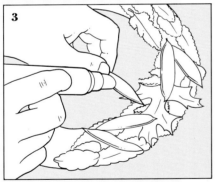

1 *Cover the cardboard ring with the least showy leaves in your collection. Apply glue sparingly to the whole underside of each leaf.*

2 *Cover the first layer of pressed leaves with others of more clearly defined shape such as scarlet oak and scarlet rowan.*

3 *Glue the seedpods at random over the leaves. For a natural look, do not plan the design symmetrically.*

To Press Leaves
Collect unblemished and undamaged fallen leaves when they are dry. Brush them lightly to remove any dust.

Arrange the leaves separately, not touching, on sheets of clean absorbent paper and cover them with another sheet of paper.

Press the leaves under pressure in a flower press, or place them between the pages of a large book such as a telephone directory under heavy weights such as a pile of more books.

Leave the press for several weeks, until the leaves are dry and brittle. Store them between tissues in boxes or airtight containers.

▲ *Colourful pheasants' feathers glued to a cardboard ring make an unusual wall decoration suitable for a hall or living room.*

◀ *Pressed leaves and dried seedpods arranged on a cardboard ring create a patchwork circlet of rich browns and greens. You can protect the decoration in a frame or under a glass tabletop.*

You will need:
Selection of pressed leaves
with as much variation of
colour and shape as possible
Dried seedpods such as lime,
sycamore or maple
A cardboard ring 25 cm
(10 in) in diameter
Clear papercraft glue

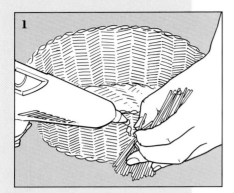

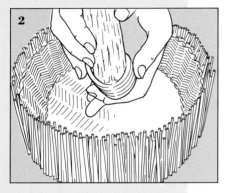

You will need:
Dry broom or other slender twigs
Roses
Florists' scissors
A shallow round box or basket
about 25 cm (10 in) across
Hot glue or clear
quick-setting glue
A stout twig about 4 cm
(1½ in) in diameter
Florists' hard-setting clay
or modelling clay
Silver roll wire
Dry moss or hay

1 *Cut short stems of twigs, just taller than the height of the container. Take handfuls of twigs and stick them all around the container, to cover the sides completely.*

2 *Cut the thick twig or branch to about 37 cm (15 in) long to represent the tree trunk. Wrap one end of it firmly with clay and fix it securely to the centre of the container base. Press on more clay if necessary to achieve a firm hold.*

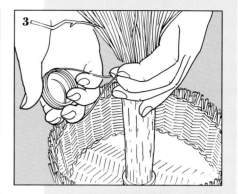

3 *Attach the silver wire close to the top of the tree trunk. Cut dry twigs to even lengths, about 15 cm (6 in) and bind them around the trunk so that they fan out at the top.*

4 *Bind on more twigs down the length of the trunk, so that each layer conceals the wire binding the one before. Secure and cut off the wire below the rim of the container. Place a little moss or hay in the container to cover the base of the trunk and the binding wire. Tuck fresh roses between the twigs composing the tree and its container.*

▲ *Twist dry but still supple twigs like clematis to form a ring and bind them with twine. Thread a napkin through the ring and tuck in one perfect rose.*

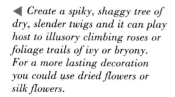

◀ *Create a spiky, shaggy tree of dry, slender twigs and it can play host to illusory climbing roses or foliage trails of ivy or bryony. For a more lasting decoration you could use dried flowers or silk flowers.*

Wayside

Scan the fields, meadows, hedgerows and waysides
for rampant weeds, dried and hollow stems, twisty
trails of ivy and field-escape cereals. They can be used
for projects ranging from child-appeal posies to a
colourful patio wreath.

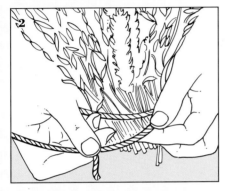

1 *Cut the oat stems to an even length so that the tips extend well beyond the rim of the container. Place the oats against the container and hold them temporarily in position with the elastic band.*

2 *When the container is covered all around with oats, tie the string around the container and remove the elastic band.*

You will need:
Flowers such as wild poppies, cornflowers and larkspur
Wild oats
Florists' scissors
A container such as an empty washed food can
Absorbent stem-holding foam, crumbled and soaked in water
An elastic band
String

▼ *Bring summer sunshine into the house on the dullest of days with this cheerful arrangement of marigolds and cornflowers in an oats-covered container.*

▶ *Arrange field poppies and cornflowers in their environmental context - in a container concealed behind a bunch of sun-dried wild oats. Because of their sap-filled stems, poppies need special treatment if they are to last well in water. Put the stems in water as soon as they are cut, and singe the end of each one with a match or candle flame before returning them at once to a moisture source.*

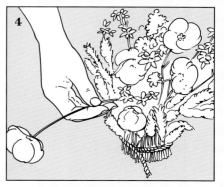

3 *Fill the container with the crumbled foam. Arrange the largest stems, of larkspur, to make a fan shape.*

4 *Arrange the poppies among the larkspur, and then position the shorter stems of cornflowers.*

Wayside

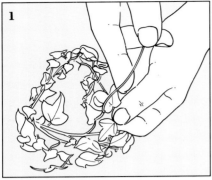

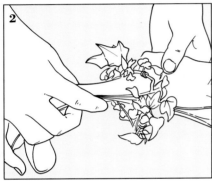

You will need:
Slender stems of small-
leaved ivy
Florists' scissors
Silver roll wire
A short, stubby twig
Florists' adhesive clay

1 *Twist two or three ivy stems together to form a ring, and bind them together with fine silver wire.*

2 *Carefully fold the napkin and push it through the ring. Arrange the napkin neatly and twist the ivy-leaf ring to ensure that the silver wire cannot be seen.*

To make the knife-rest, twist a short, slender stem of small-leaved ivy around the twig and secure the ends at the back with small dabs of clay.

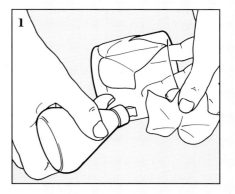

1

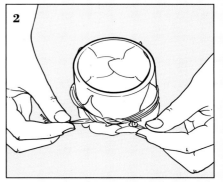

2

You will need:
A straight-sided tumbler
Large ivy leaves
Clear papercraft glue
Raffia

1 *Select three or four leaves that will form a continuous decoration when glued side by side around the tumbler. Spread the glue sparingly over the back of each leaf and press it onto the tumbler.*

2 *Gather several strands of raffia together and cut the ends evenly. Tie the raffia band around the tumbler and tie a knot.*

▲ *Make the most of the ivy-leaf containers by choosing short, stubby candles. These beehive-shaped ones are made of sweet-smelling beeswax.*

◀ *Take three slender, sword-shaped iris leaves, knot them around a fanned-out linen napkin and tuck in a yellow iris flower for a simple and stylish table decoration.*

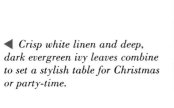

◀ *Crisp white linen and deep, dark evergreen ivy leaves combine to set a stylish table for Christmas or party-time.*

Wayside

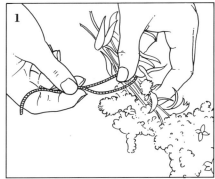

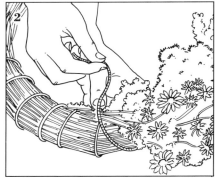

You will need:
Selection of wayside plant
materials such as rosebay
willowherb, ragwort,
meadowsweet, feverfew,
burdock and thistles
A vine twig ring 30 cm
(12 in) in diameter
Florists' scissors
Green twine

1 *Cut the flowers and seedhead
stems to equal length. Bind three
or four stems of each type into
separate bunches.*

2 *Fasten one end of the twine to
the wreath base, and bind the
bunches onto it so that the heads
of each one cover the stem ends of
the previous one. Continue until
the ring is completely covered.*

▶ *Wild flowers or weeds, call
them what you will, wayside
stems can be used for an outdoor
decoration pretty enough to set
the scene for a party in the
garden.*

Care of Wild Flowers

You may be able to gather wild flowers from your own or a friend's garden. If that is not possible, be sure to cut only rampant weeds from the wayside. It is forbidden to cut all other wild plants.

Many wild flowers are more delicate or more likely to wilt than cultivated forms. Put the stems in water as soon as possible after they have been cut. Bind them into bunches and leave these in water until just before you want to hang the decoration. It takes only a few minutes to bind the bunches onto the ring. Spray the ring with cool water, and do this at frequent intervals if the weather is hot or humid.

Wayside

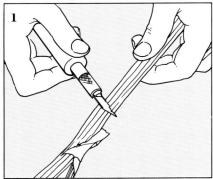

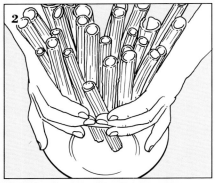

1 *Cut the dried hogweed stems so that they will extend about 5 cm (2 in) above the rim of the container. Use a very sharp-bladed knife to avoid splitting.*

2 *Gather the stems in a bundle, twist them slightly so that they settle at an angle, and lower them into the container.*

3 *Arrange dried foliage and flowers in the hollow stems to form the shape of a fan.*

You will need:
Dried hogweed stems
A craft knife
A wide-necked glass container
Selection of brightly coloured
dried flowers such as bleached
and dyed ruscus leaves
and bottlebrush
Florists' scissors

▶ *Giant hogweed stems, with their rough texture and hollow centres, are bunched together to make a cluster of stem vases. They look equally dramatic with dried or fresh flowers.*

► *Conceal orchid phials or other water-holding containers in hogweed stems, and choose the brightest flowers you can to contrast dramatically with the natural stem vases.*

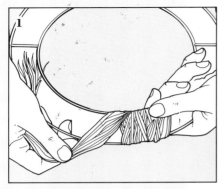

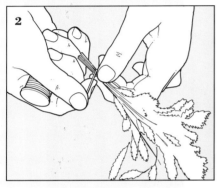

You will need:
Wild grasses
Wild poppies
Florists' scissors
A double wire ring frame
25 cm (10 in) in diameter
Raffia
Silver roll wire
Binding twine

1 *Take about ten strands of raffia, knot them together at one end and tie them to the wire frame. Bind the frame with raffia, joining on more as necessary, until it is covered all round.*

2 *Form the grasses into small bunches, cut the stems level and bind them with silver wire.*

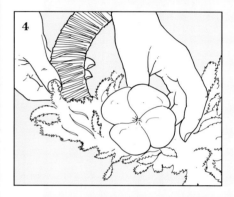

3 Bind the bunches to the raffia-covered frame so that the heads of one bunch cover the stems of the one before. Reverse the last bunch to neaten the appearance.

4 For a short-term splash of colour, tuck wild poppies or other bright flowers in among the grasses.

◀ The contrasting sizes of linseed (flax) and poppy seedheads make an interesting composition on a wreath base made of grass stems.

▲ Gather decorative field grasses into bunches, bind them to a ring frame and, for a burst of colour, tuck in a handful of poppies. The grasses will gradually fade from the palest green to a sun-bleached gold. For how to keep poppies looking fresh see page 40.

▶ *Verdigris candle sconces with a wheat-ear design are enhanced by a simple stook of wheat stalks made in a similar way to the flowerpot arrangement. Gather the stalks loosely in one hand, twist them sharply between your thumb and first finger and bind them just beneath the heads with a few strands of raffia.*

▶ *These two arrangements feature wheat just the way it grows, with the large, closely packed ears erect on tall, upright stems. They show how a handful of 'field escape' stems gathered by the wayside can become stylish decorations in a matter of minutes.*

1 Cut the wheat stalks to about 45 cm (18 in) long. Hold one in your hand and arrange a circle of others around it, with the heads at a slightly lower level. Arrange another ring around those, with the heads lower than the previous ones and so on until the bunch is the size you wish. Hold the stems in place with an elastic band and tie several strands of raffia over it. Tie into a knot and cut off the ends. Bind the stalks lower down with more raffia and cut the ends level.

2 Wrap a strip of clay around the stalk ends and press it firmly into the centre of the flowerpot. Check that the bunch is held securely, and add more clay if necessary. Scatter a handful of dry hay or moss in the pot to conceal the fixing.

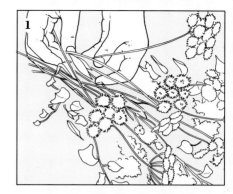

Flat-backed Sheaf
You will need:
Selection of long-stemmed
materials such as ivy, sheep's
parsley or wild carrot
and grasses
Flowers such as marguerites
and cornflowers
Florists' scissors
Raffia

1 *Arrange the long-stemmed foliage and flowers flat on a working surface, so that the heads fan slightly outwards.*

2 *Cut the flower stems in graduating lengths and arrange them over the first layer. Bind the stems with raffia and cut the stem ends level.*

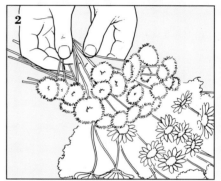

Hand-arranged Posy
You will need:
Selection of flowers such as red
campions, marguerites,
buttercups and cornflowers
Oats or barley
Leaves such as buttercup
Raffia
Florists' scissors

1 *Arrange the flowers in one hand, the stems of those around the outside progressively shorter than those in the centre.*

2 *Arrange the ring of oats around the flowers and include a few buttercup leaves on short stems. Bind the stems with raffia and cut the stem ends level.*

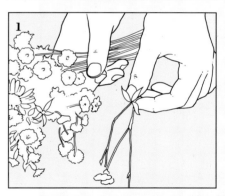

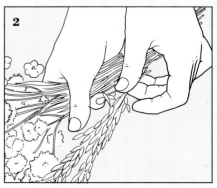

◀ ▲ *Victorian-style posies arranged in the hand or cascades of flowers and foliage composed flat on a table; both make delightful gifts for town or city-dwelling friends.*

Put the flowers and foliage in water as soon as you cut them and immediately after you have arranged them. If you are taking the posy as a gift, wrap the stem ends in damp tissues and seal the arrangement in a large polyethylene bag to keep it moist.

Country Garden

Cauliflowers and corncobs from the vegetable patch, herbs gathered from pots on the windowsill, glistening strawberries and fragrant flowers - whatever your garden harvest, it has decorative nature craft potential.

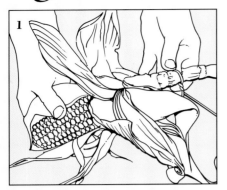

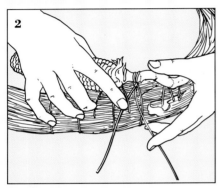

1 Spray pear-shaped gourds and leave them to dry. Twist a stub wire tightly around the stalk of each one and twist the two ends of the wire together. Pull back some of the dried corn leaves to reveal the corncobs. Twist a stub wire firmly around the stalk of each cob and twist the two ends of the wire together. As a further fixing of the two outside cobs, twist two stub wires together to form a longer length and wrap that around the cob, where it will be concealed by the leaves. Twist the wire ends together at the back.

2 Secure the corncobs by pressing the wires into the stem ring and bending back the ends on the reverse of the ring. Attach the gold-sprayed gourds similarly. It may be necessary to use a little glue to hold the gourds firmly in place. Stick the small unsprayed gourds to the base of the wreath.

You will need:
Dried decorative corncobs
Dried gourds
Gold spray paint
Small dried gourds
A stem wreath form
25 cm (10 in) in diameter
Heavy-gauge stub wires
Wirecutters
Hot glue or
clear quick-setting glue

◀ *The kitchen garden provides the produce and inspiration for this unusual autumnal wealth. The decoration is composed of dried decorative corncobs and dried gourds sprayed shining gold.*

▶ *Asparagus and spring onions (scallions), beetroot and carrots, green beans and radishes, this colourful garden produce is all bunched up with raffia and wired to a stem wreath base. A few fresh herbs tucked in among the vegetables give the design a refreshing straight-from-the-garden aroma.*

Country Garden

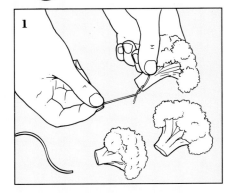

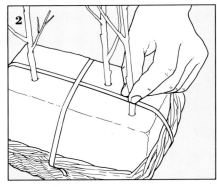

1 *Cut the broccoli and cauliflower into florets. Cut the stub wires in half. Thread a wire through each broccoli and cauliflower floret and twist the two ends together. Wire the button mushrooms and garlic heads in a similar way.*

2 *Wedge a piece of soaked foam to fit firmly in the basket and secure it with two crossing strips of florists' adhesive tape. Position short lengths of twigs at widely spaced intervals in the foam.*

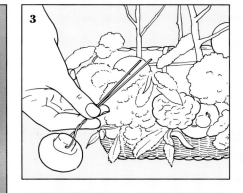

3 *Position wired broccoli and cauliflower florets, heads of garlic and mushrooms around the rim of the basket to cover the foam. Position sprigs of mint between the vegetables to fill in the spaces.*

4 *Arrange long stems of lilies to form a straight line across the top of the design. Cut the rose stems so that when they are positioned they will fill the gap between the vegetables and the lilies. Position more sprigs of mint to fill any spaces.*

◀ *Cauliflower, broccoli, garlic, mint, roses and lilies arranged together in a rectangular basket comprise a two-colour design that would be perfect for a formal dinner party.*

You will need:
Knobbly twigs such as
apple wood
1 small firm cauliflower
1 head of green broccoli
Dried garlic
Button mushrooms
Variegated mint
White roses

White lilies
A rectangular basket
Polyethylene sheet liner
Absorbent stem-holding foam
Florists' adhesive tape
Stub wires
Wirecutters
Florists' scissors

Country Garden

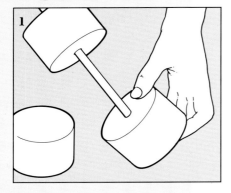

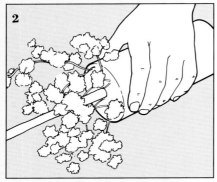

You will need:
Selection of flowers such as
lady's mantle, marguerites,
roses, feverfew, marigolds and
Geranium wallichianum
Florists' scissors
Thin garden cane
3 Cylinders of absorbent
stem-holding foam,
soaked in water
Strips of paper ribbon

1 *Mark the centres of the foam cylinders and push them close together on the cane. If necessary, wrap a stub wire beneath the last one to keep it from slipping.*

2 *Cut short sprays of lady's mantle and push them into the underside of the lowest cylinder so that the stems hang vertically.*

▶ *Light up a terrace or patio, doorway or porch with a floral 'beacon' that will glow well after nightfall. You can even position the decorations on the lawn or in a shrub border to create instant colour and impact.*

Country Garden

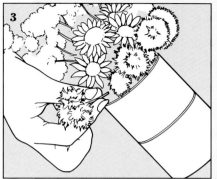

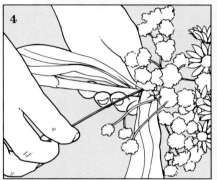

3 *Cut short stems of the other flowers and push them into the foam to form rings all around the decoration. Continue to the top of the foam and create a mound effect with lady's mantle.*

4 *Hold the ribbon strips against the cane just below the foam and bind them in place with stub wires. Ease the ribbons so that they are evenly spaced around the cane. Spray the flowers with cold water to keep them looking fresh for as long as possible.*

Country Garden

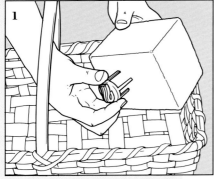

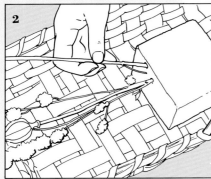

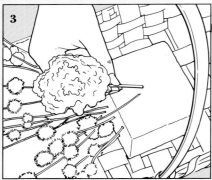

You will need:
Dried flowers such as larkspur,
delphinium, rosebuds, lavender,
peony, cornflowers, pink
everlastings and strawflowers
Dried poppy and
love-in-a-mist seedheads
Dried grasses, wheat and
wheat stalks
A shallow basket about
37 x 22 cm (15 x 9 in)
Florists' scissors
A four-pronged plastic spike
Florists' adhesive clay
Block of dry stem-holding foam
Medium-gauge stub wires
Wirecutters
Paper ribbon in two colours

◀ *The fragrance of dried ruby
red and yellow rose petals,
lavender and variegated mint
leaves is enhanced by the subtle
addition of powdered spices
and a couple of drops of attar
of roses oil. The colourful
blend is displayed in a
bronze-look papier-mâché
dish.*

1 *Press a strip of adhesive clay to
the base of the plastic prong and
press it into the basket, just to one
side of the handle.*

2 *Position the longest stems of
the dried materials, delphiniums,
larkspur and wheat.*

3 *Position progressively shorter
stems, with large flowers pressed
close against the foam near the
handle. Fill in the design with
contrasting flowers, taking care
to avoid a crowded look.*

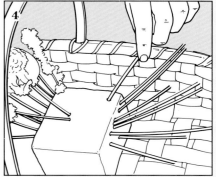

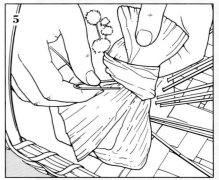

4 Cut wheat stalks to varying lengths between about 10-15 cm (4-6 in). Arrange these in a fan shape in the exposed side of the foam, to represent stalks of the arranged flowers.

5 Tie a two-loop bow with two colours of paper ribbon (see instructions on page 21) and bind the centre with a short length of wire. Bend half a stub wire into a U-shaped staple, push it through the wire at the back of the bow and press it into the foam. Arrange a few more flowers on short stems to cover any area of the foam that is still visible.

◀ A shallow Shaker basket arranged with a medley of colourful dried flowers makes a delightful gift, or a charming 'bouquet' for a bride and her attendants to carry.

Country Garden

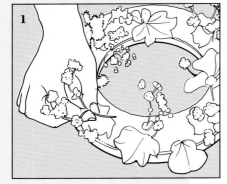

You will need:
Flowers such as lady's mantle,
Geranium wallichianum,
cornflowers and roses
About 250 g (8 oz)
ripe strawberries
Wooden toothpicks or
cocktail sticks
Florists' scissors
A stem-holding foam ring
25 cm (10 in) in diameter,
soaked in water

1 *Cut short sprays of lady's mantle and arrange them around the ring. Position some of the leaves close against the foam, to conceal it.*

2 *Arrange the geraniums and cornflowers in clusters, as if they are growing in patches in the garden, then arrange the roses between them.*

▲ *Freshly picked raspberries arranged on a bed of lady's mantle in a small trug - simply too tempting!*

▶ *Glistening, gleaming strawberries just on the point of ripeness are not only delicious, they are decorative too. Here they are arranged in clusters in a table centre ring of flowers from a country garden.*

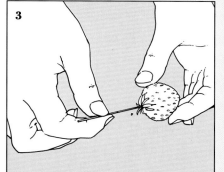

3 Spear the strawberries on the wooden sticks, piercing some at the stalk end and others at the base.

4 Arrange the strawberries in two clusters, at opposite sides of the ring, and have a few replacements ready in case any guests find them irresistible. Spray the flowers and fruit with cool water at intervals, especially if the decoration is left in full sun.

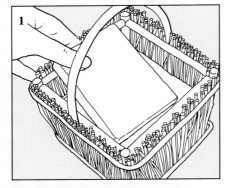

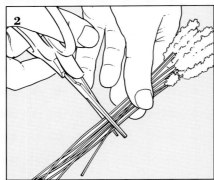

1 Cut the foam to fit the base of the basket and put it in place.

2 Measure the required height of the lavender - the heads extend about 4 cm (1½ in) above the basket rim - and cut the stems to length.

3 Cut the rose stems to an equal length and position them in a line through the centre of the basket, beneath the handle.

You will need:
A straight-sided basket about
20 cm (8 in) square
Lavender
About 8 dried rosebuds
Florists' scissors
A piece of dry stem-holding
foam about 4 cm (1½ in) thick
A knife
Raffia plait
Medium-gauge stub wires

◀ *Tightly packed lavender flowers and a neat row of dried rosebuds arranged in a gypsy basket add up to a look of pure nostalgia.*

▶ *Turn the design concept on its side and arrange the lavender stems horizontally in a small trug, on either side of a double row of rosebuds. This design is pretty for a dressing table or bedside table.*

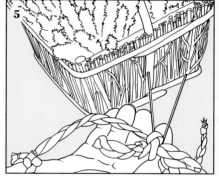

4 Take small bunches of lavender, about ten stems at a time, and press them vertically into the foam. Continue until the lavender fills the basket.

5 Tie the raffia plait into a bow. Bend the stub wire in half and thread it through the back of the loop. Push the wires through the basket and bend back the ends to secure the bow.

Country Garden

▲ *This rosehip wreath enhanced with some late blooms on a twisted twig ring makes an attractive end-of-summer decoration with a suggestion of the fruitful season to come.*

You will need:
Fresh herb foliage such as sage,
purple sage, marjoram,
variegated mint, woodruff
Flowers such as pansies, pinks,
cornflowers, love-in-a-mist,
marigolds, roses,
lady's mantle, feverfew
A double wire ring frame
25 cm (10 in) in diameter
Dry hay or sphagnum moss
Green twine
Silver roll wire
Florists' scissors
Medium-gauge stub wires
Wirecutters

▶ *A heart-shaped wreath of fresh herb flower posies has more than a hint of romance. You can compose the tiny nosegays in advance of a special occasion and keep them in water.*

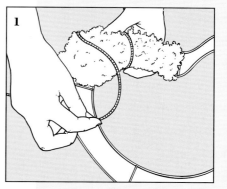

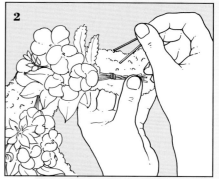

1 *Bend the wire frame into a heart shape, pinching it at both ends. Tie the twine to the ring shape. Take small handfuls of the hay or moss and bind them to the frame. Continue until the frame is completely covered with the dry material. Fasten the twine to the frame.*

2 *Form the foliage and flowers into posies and bind the stem with fine silver wire. Cut stub wires in half and bend them into U-shaped staples. Attach each posy to the frame by pushing a staple over the stems. Bend back the wire ends behind the frame to secure them. Continue around the frame, positioning the posies so that the heads of one cover the stems of the one before.*
　　To keep the fresh-flower decoration looking at its best for as long as possible, spray it frequently with cool water and hang it in a cool airy room away from direct sunlight.

Country Garden

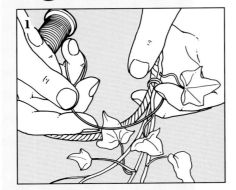

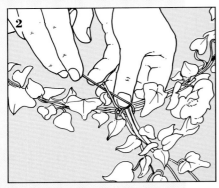

1 *Measure the coiled paper or other core material around the edge of the table and cut it a little longer, to allow for overlapping. Tie the roll wire to one end of the core, overlap the ends and bind them together to make a circle. Taking two or three ivy stems together, according to their size, bind them to the core, concealing the wire behind the leaves. Add more stems until the core is covered all the way round.*

2 *Cut off the rose stems and stick the roses at intervals around the garland. For the small table in the photograph, the roses were spaced 10 cm (4 in) apart. Choose two or three branching stems of ivy to make a central feature. Glue on a few more roses and bind the stems at right angles to the garland. Bind a spray of roses over the join.*

◀ *Edge a party table with a garland of ivy and roses to give it a pretty and festive effect. The ivy trails are bound to a core of coiled paper ribbon colour co-ordinated to the roses.*

To give the garland the freshest possible look, you may like to bind the ivy trails the night before the event or early in the morning and stick on the roses before the start. Lightly crush the rose stems and keep them in water until it is time to attach them to the decoration.

You will need:
Long trails of small-leaved ivy
Roses
Coiled paper ribbon, or
string or cord
Silver roll wire
Hot glue or
clear quick-setting glue
Florists' scissors

▲ *It's roses all the way for this casual hat trim. Bind the flowers and leaves to make two small posies and fix them to the hat with stub wire staples pushed through the straw.*

Market Stall

Yield to the market-stall temptation of aromatic spices,
zingy citrus fruits, exotic seedheads, and other
decorative foods from faraway places and you have a
wealth of possibilities for the most imaginative
of projects.

Market Stall

1

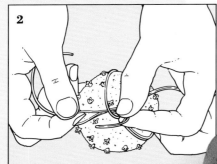

2

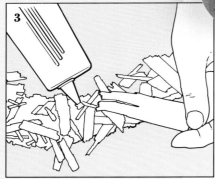

3

1 *Stud the oranges, limes and lemon with the cloves. If the fruit rind is specially tough it may be necessary to pierce it first with a darning needle or fine skewer.*

2 *Tie the citrus pomanders with the leather thonging, finishing with a small bow.*

3 *Cover the lower half of the stem ring with cinnamon bark or shavings, gluing the strips randomly at all angles.*

You will need:
2 Oranges
2 Limes
1 Lemon
Cloves
A darning needle or fine
skewer (optional)
Narrow leather thonging
Long cinnamon sticks
Raffia
Cinnamon bark or 'shavings',
from Asian grocers
Exotic seedheads such as brazil
nut cases, from florists
Sprays of bay leaves
A twisted twig ring
25 cm (10 in) in diameter
Medium-gauge stub wires
Wirecutters
Florists' scissors
Hot glue or
clear quick-setting glue

► *Turn back the clock to the Middle Ages when homes were scented with 'clove oranges' and bunches of fragrant herbs. This tangy citrus fruit and mixed spice ring has more than just a refreshing aroma - it is highly decorative too.*

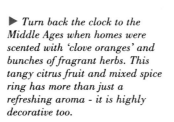

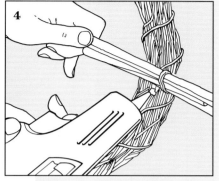

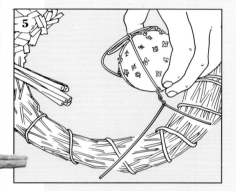

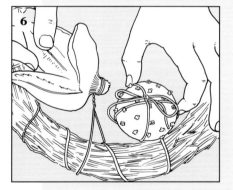

4 *Tie the cinnamon sticks into equal bundles with the raffia and glue them across the centre of the ring or fix them to the ring with a bent stub wire staple .*

5 *Push stub wires through the back of each fruit, twist the two ends of the wire and attach it to the ring.*

6 *Wire or glue the seedheads in place. Wire sprays of bay leaves on either side of the ring.*

Market Stall

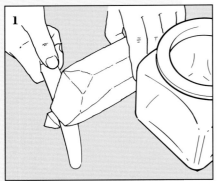

1 *Cut the foam into a near-cylindrical shape, to stand in the centre of the jar and extend about 4 cm (1½ in) above the rim. Press a strip of adhesive clay to the base of the plastic spike, press it onto the base of the jar and push the foam onto it.*

2 *Fill the space between the foam and the jar with kidney beans. Tap the jar firmly to allow the beans to settle and top up with more if necessary.*

▶ *A kitchen jar apparently filled with dried red kidney beans becomes a high-profile container for a collection of exotic seedcases and dried leaves. You could make a similar arrangement in a jar layered with spices instead of kidney beans.*

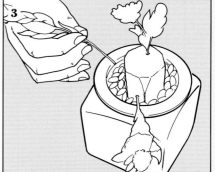

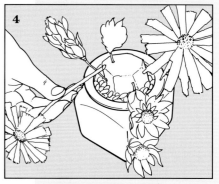

You will need:
Bleached and dyed leaves
such as ruscus
Exotic seedcases such as brazil
nut cases, heart-shaped flor de
Madeira pods and sea-urchin-
like pods of *Girasol espinol*
Angular twigs
Dried flowers such as *Protea*
'Supercut' and red bottlebrush
A glass container about
20 cm (8 in) high
Dry stem-holding foam
A knife
A four-pronged plastic spike
Florists' adhesive clay
Florists' scissors
Dried red kidney beans
A spoon
Medium-gauge stub wires
Wirecutters

◄ *Coriander seeds, juniper berries and red peppercorns arranged in layers make a colourful and aromatic kitchen decoration, and one which would make an unusual gift.*

▼ *Three of the dried materials featured in the floral arrangement are, left to right, Protea 'Supercut' flower, Girasol espinol and a brazil nut case, which is imported from the Amazon.*
Many of the exotic seedcases are sold with no stalks and will need to be mounted on wires to create false stems. (See Wiring Techniques on pages 14-15).

3 Position the sprays of dyed leaves with some stems slanting outwards on either side of the container, and others pointing outwards.

4 Arrange one of the largest items, in this case a Protea 'Supercut', as a central feature, where it will become the focal point of the design. Arrange the twigs and other dried materials around it, taking care that the stem-holding foam is completely concealed.

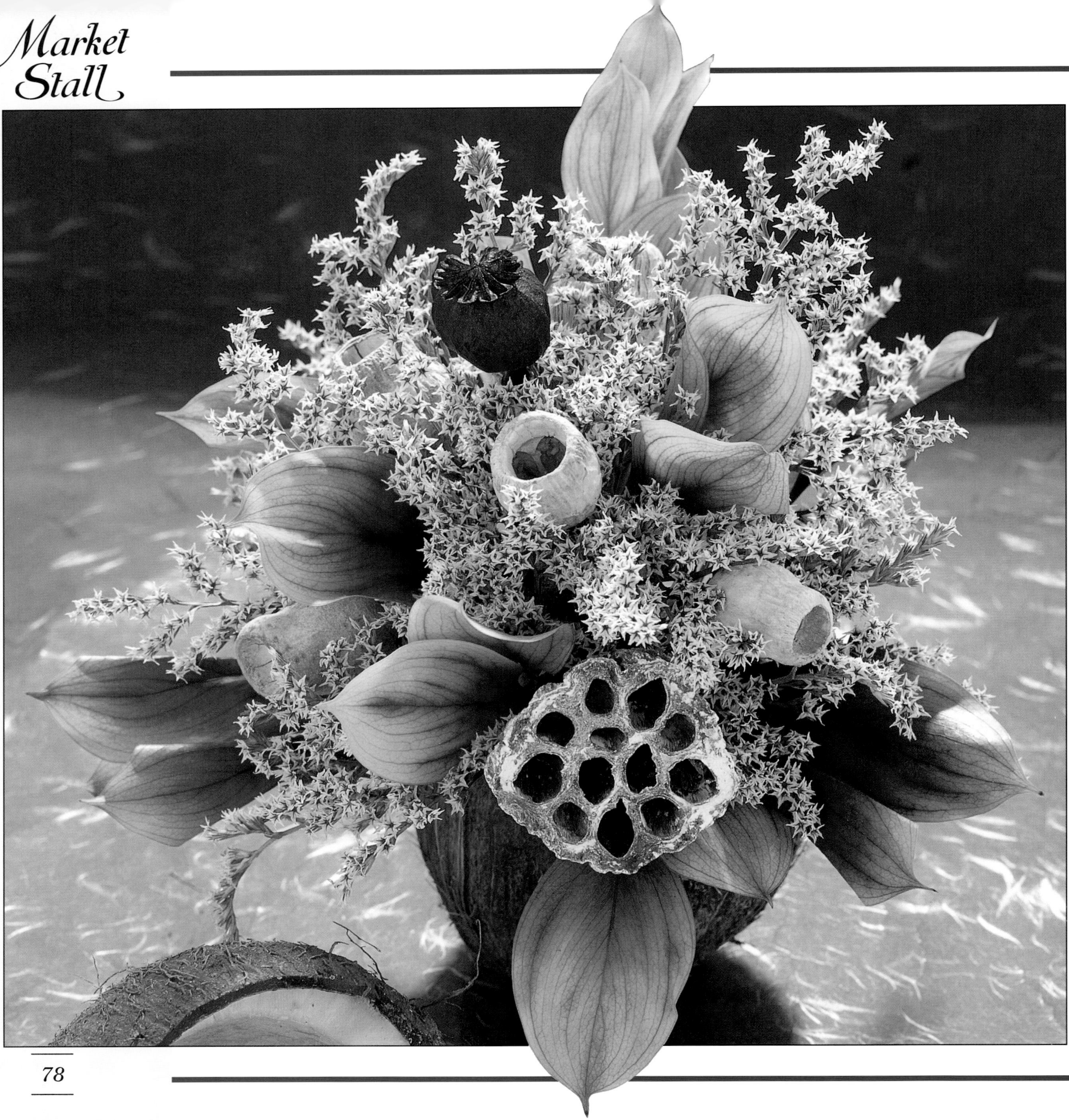

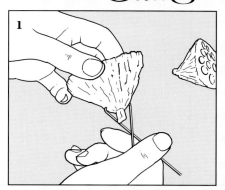

1 *The lotus seedpods, which are often sold without the stems, are whitened with emulsion paint to give them a bleached look. First push a stub wire through the seedpod close to the base. Cross the two ends of the wire and twist them together to form a false stem.*

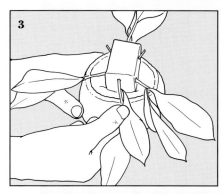

2 *Hold each seedpod over the paint container and use the brush to work the paint deep into the crevices. Shake off the excess paint and place the seedpods on newspaper to dry.*

3 *Saw a slice from the top of the coconut and drain off the milk. Saw a thin slice from the base so that it stands level. Cut a piece of dry foam to fit tightly in the top. Push stub wires through the foam and into the coconut to keep the foam in place. Cut short lengths of foliage and arrange them in the foam to form a rough triangular shape. Position some leaves to slant low over the coconut rim.*

◀ *Contrast bleached and dyed foliage such as ruscus leaves with silver-grey sea lavender, and exotic seedpods with home-grown poppy heads. Arrange them together in a half coconut shell and you have a flamboyant design in party mood.*

You will need:
Lotus seedpods
Medium-gauge stub wires
White emulsion paint
diluted with water
A small paintbrush
Colourful foliage
Poppy and other seedheads
Sea lavender
A coconut shell
A saw
Florists' scissors
Dry stem-holding foam
A knife

▲ *Whitened lotus heads and pine cones nestle among sprays of silver-grey and blue-dyed sea lavender in an old stone pot. Here is a near-monochromatic arrangement that would look well in a room furnished mainly in grey or white.*

4 *Position the seedpods to follow the outline of the leaves. Place one of the whitened lotus heads low over the rim of the coconut. Position short sprays of sea lavender to fill in the gaps and to cover the foam at the back of the arrangement.*

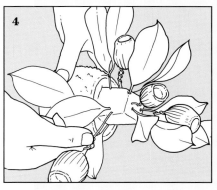

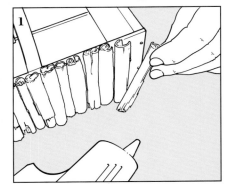

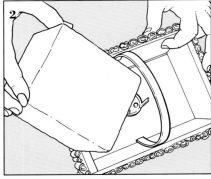

You will need:
Cinnamon sticks
Red and green chillies
Bay leaves
Heads of garlic
Limes
A straight-sided wooden basket
about 20 cm (8 in) long
Hot glue or
clear quick-setting glue
A four-pronged plastic spike
Florists' adhesive clay
Dry stem-holding foam
A knife
Florists' scissors
Medium-gauge stub wires
Wirecutters

1 *Cut the cinnamon sticks so that they come just above the rim of the basket. Stick them close together to cover the basket all round.*

2 *Cut the block of foam so that it fits tightly in the basket and extends about 2.5 cm (1 in) above the top of the cinnamon sticks.*

▲ *This brown-on-brown kitchen decoration is made by gluing cinnamon sticks to a cardboard shape, with a raffia bow and a Protea 'Supercut' flower added for maximum impact. A smaller version decorated with, for example, a cluster of small larch cones would make a stylish parcel trim.*

▶ *A small wooden basket gets the log-cabin look with a covering of cinnamon sticks. It gets a new cargo, too - a blaze of red and green chillies, heads of garlic and tangy limes.*

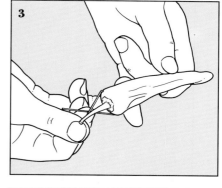

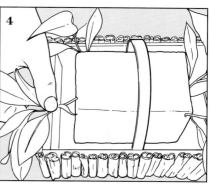

3 To wire the chillies, push a wire through just below the stalk. Twist the two ends of the wire together close to the stalk. Wire the heads of garlic and the limes in a similar way.

4 Arrange short sprays of bay leaves around the basket, with some trailing low over the rim. Position the cinnamon sticks diagonally on each side of the basket, with some shorter ones at the front. Position the wired chillies, garlic and limes between them, and check that the foam is completely concealed.

81

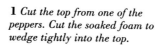

You will need:
4 or 5 Red bell peppers
Red poppies
Marigolds
Deep pink flowers such as
sweet William and pinks
Maple leaves
A shallow straight-sided basket
A small piece of absorbent
stem-holding foam
A knife
Dry hay or sphagnum moss
Florists' scissors

◀ *A basket of red bell peppers entwined with maple leaves has the added vibrancy of a cluster of scarlet poppies, marigolds and carmine pinks - a design to match the heat of summer.*

1 *Cut the top from one of the peppers. Cut the soaked foam to wedge tightly into the top.*

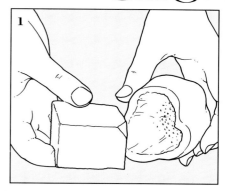

2 *Line the base of the basket with hay or moss. Arrange the whole peppers in the basket, stem sides down, and the pepper vase with the foam extending just above the rim.*

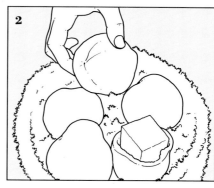

3 *Push the stemlets of the leaves into the basket so that the foliage appears to be wrapped around the sides.*

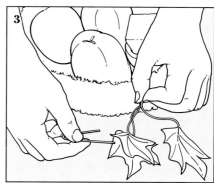

4 *Arrange the smaller flowers in the foam so that some of them overlap the basket rim. Cut short the poppy stems and position them in the foam so that the heads come just above the top of the peppers.*

▲ Colour-match your pot pourri to your furnishing scheme and it becomes an eye-catching accessory. This blue and cream blend includes dried cornflowers, hydrangea florets, lavender, larkspur, sea lavender, marjoram flowers, strawflowers and tansy. The added fragrances are ground ginger and cinnamon, with rosemary oil and the fixative, ground orris root powder.

Drying Plant Materials
Gather petals and flowers for drying on a dry day, and discard any blemished or damaged ones. Spread them in a single layer on a tray or in a shallow basket and dry them outside in partial shade - the traditional way - or in an airing cupboard or other warm,

dry place. Stir the materials frequently until they feel and sound as crisp as cornflakes.

You can also add any already dried flowers and leaves to your pot pourri blend. It is a satisfying way to use off-cuts and snippings from larger arrangements in a further decorative way.

▶ Making pot pourri offers you the chance to combine petals and flowers from the garden, moss and cones from the countryside and exotic and lingering aromas from the spice market. The blends shown on these pages are chosen as much for their texture and colour appeal as for their distinctive fragrances.

Green Moss Pot Pourri

1 Cup deep red dried peony
or rose petals
1 Cup dried green moss
½ Cup dried eucalyptus leaves
A few *Nigella orientalis*
seedheads
1 tbsp Coriander seeds,
lightly crushed
1 tsp Allspice seeds,
lightly crushed
1 tsp Ground cinnamon
1 tbsp Ground orris root powder
2 Drops geranium oil,
or other essential oil

*Put all the plant materials and
spices into a large container, stir
well, and add the ground orris
root powder, the fixative that will
'hold' the other fragrances. Cover
the jar and set it aside, away
from direct sunlight, for 1 week,
stirring the contents every day.
Add the oil and set aside for a
further 5 weeks, stirring each day
if possible.*

Whole Spice Blend

1 Cup small pine or larch cones
1 Cup dried bay leaves,
lightly crumbled
1 Cup dried pine leaves
½ Cup dried rosehips
½ Cup dried eucalyptus leaves
1 tbsp Coriander seeds
2 tbsp Star anise seedpods
1 tbsp Juniper berries
1 tsp Cloves
2 Cinnamon sticks, crumbled
4-5 Nutmegs
A few blades of mace
Dried peel of 1 orange
3 Drops pine oil or orange oil

*Mix together all the plant
materials and spices so that they
are well blended. Add the
essential oil, and mix well. Set
the mixture aside in a lidded
container for 6 weeks, stirring it
every day if possible.*

Market Stall

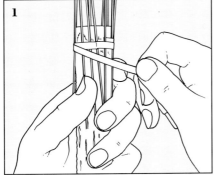

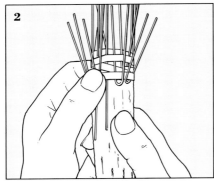

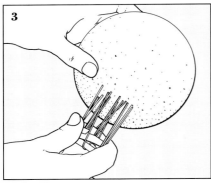

1 *Place a few stub wires close together around the top of the twig, with half their length extending above it. Bind these wires in place and add more, binding them securely.*

2 *Bend back the lower half of the wires over the band of adhesive tape, to double the number around the top.*

3 *Push the foam ball onto the circle of wires so that it is held firmly in place.*

◀ *Everyday ingredients like peanuts, walnuts and bunches of cinnamon, and even an old earthenware flowerpot, can be transformed with a puff of gold spray paint. This spice ball tree would make a festive centrepiece at Christmas time.*

Tie short lengths of cinnamon sticks into criss-crossing bunches, and spatter-spray them and some of the nuts with gold paint. Cut short lengths of stub wires. Pierce the peanut shells with a wire, glue wires to the walnuts and pecans, and loop a wire around the raffia to tie the cinnamon bunches. We left the pecan shells unsprayed, to give a contrast of colour and texture, and chose gossamer ribbon in a toning shade.

You will need:
Selection of nuts such as peanuts
in the shell, walnuts and pecans
Cinnamon sticks
Raffia
Gold spray paint
Gossamer ribbon 4 cm
(1½ in) wide
A stout twig about 20 cm
(8 in) long
Medium or heavy-gauge
stub wires
Florists' adhesive tape
Dry sphagnum moss
A flowerpot about 12.5 cm
(5 in) in diameter
A dry foam ball 17.5 cm
(7 in) in diameter
Hard-setting clay or
modelling clay
Florists' scissors
Hot glue or
clear quick-setting glue

4

5

4 *Fix the stick in the pot with clay. Cut some wires in half and bend them to make U-shaped staples. Take small handfuls of the moss and attach it to the foam ball, holding it in place with the staples.*

5 *Decorate the foam ball with wired nuts and cinnamon sticks (see caption to the illustration). Tie a ribbon bow around the stick just beneath the ball, and fill the pot with moss.*

87

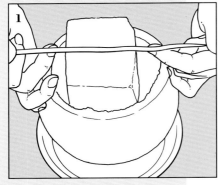

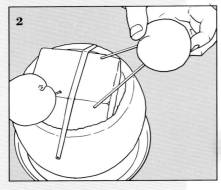

1 *Cut away the flesh from the watermelon and scoop it out with a spoon. Take care not to pierce the shell of the fruit. Cut the block of soaked foam to fit inside the shell of the fruit, so that it extends about 4 cm (1½ in) above the rim. Put it in place and secure it with a strip of adhesive tape crossing over from side to side.*

2 *Pierce each of the nectarines with two cocktail sticks or toothpicks positioned to make a V shape. Insert the sticks into the foam so that the fruit rests close to the rim of the watermelon.*

You will need:
1 Watermelon
Flowers such as lisianthus
and sweet peas
3 Nectarines
Florists' scissors
A knife
A spoon
Absorbent stem-holding foam,
soaked in water
Florists' adhesive tape
Wooden cocktail sticks or
toothpicks

▶ *Colourful or exotic fruits and vegetables make unusual short-term containers. You can scoop out the flesh and include it in the dinner-party menu, or add a slice of fruit as a glistening accessory to the group.*

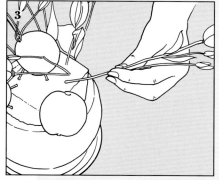

3 *Arrange the longest stems of flowers, in this case purple lisianthus, at the back of the container. Cut some stems short and position them between the nectarines.*

4 *Fill in the design with sweet peas, alternating the light and dark colours to give variety throughout the design.*

Seashore

Comb the beaches for shells and sea lavender, dried seaweed and scraps of discarded rope. Look for decorative materials that may be craggy and rugged or pearly and elegant, to recapture the tantalizing tang of the sea.

Seashore

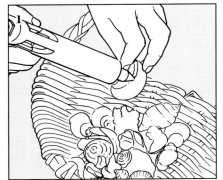

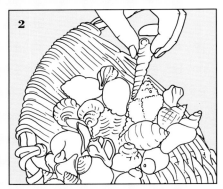

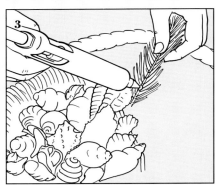

1 *Glue the shells close together, alternating the shapes and hues to give the collage clear definition.*

2 *Glue cone-shaped shells such as augers to form a fan shape at the top of the collage.*

3 *Glue short lengths of coral, positioning them as if they are arranged in the auger 'vases'. Lastly, glue on a small piece of seaweed to provide a contrast in texture.*

◄ *Glue shells and shell slices onto wooden toothpicks and display them in a large decorative shell filled with soft light brown 'sand' sugar.*

You will need:
A woven basket shape about 30 cm (12 in) across
Selection of shells
3 small pieces of coral
A small piece of dried seaweed
Hot glue or clear quick-setting glue

► *A woven basket shape, which you can buy from florists, takes on a nautical look with a collage of shells, coral and seaweed.*

▼ *A cuttlefish makes a perfect foundation for a glossy collage of small and prettily - shaped marginella and slipper shells.*

Seashore

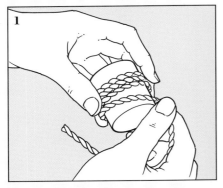

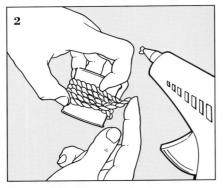

You will need:
Shiny dressing-gown cord
Selection of small shells
Egg cup or cardboard tube about
6 cm (2¾ in) in diameter
Hot glue or
clear quick-setting glue

1 *Using an egg cup or a piece of cardboard tube as a core, and starting at about 20 cm (8 in) from one end of the cord, wind it around the core five times, pushing the strands close together and gluing them in place. Cut off and glue the second end of the cord.*

2 *Angle the long, loose end of the cord diagonally across the band and glue it in position.*

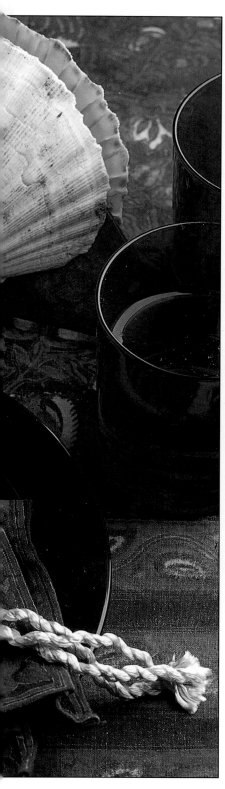

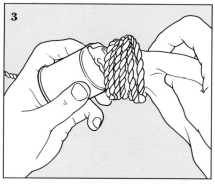

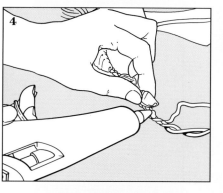

◀ *Give your table a nautical look by using shells in a variety of ways, as candle holders, napkin holders and to decorate napkin rings made of shiny cord.*

▲ *Display a collection of sea-washed shells and pebbles on a plain dish to emphasize the variety of their colours and patterns. A tactile decoration like this is designed to be constantly handled and rearranged.*

3 *Slip the cord band off the egg cup or other core material onto a folded napkin.*

4 *Glue small shells to the cord diagonal and to the free end. Unravel the last 5 cm (2 in) of the cord. The last shell will prevent further unravelling.*

Craggy shells with their pearlized interiors make pretty reflectors for night-lights. Group several together in the centre of the table, or place one beside each setting. Select two scallop shells which are evenly matched for size and glue them together at the base to make a stylish napkin holder. The decoration can also be used to hold writing paper and envelopes, or as an invoice tidy.

Seashore

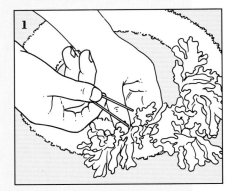

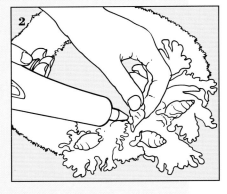

1 *Cut some stub wires in half and bend them to make U-shaped staples. Use them to attach sprays of seaweed to the stem ring.*

2 *Glue small shells such as turrids to the clusters of seaweed, to look as if they are caught up in the plant.*

▶ *A bright yellow cowrie shell becomes the centre of attention in a holiday collection. The traditional preserving jar, a functional and effective container, is back-lit through a window.*

3 *Using the wire staples, attach short lengths of coral to follow the line of the ring base.*

4 *Attach clumps of a contrasting seaweed to cover the bare stems of the coral. Finish the design by gluing on more shells.*

You will need:
2 Species of dried seaweed
Short lengths of
coral shells of different shapes
and sizes
Stem ring 25 cm
(10 in) in diameter
Hot glue or
clear quick-setting glue
Medium-gauge stub wires
Wirecutters
Florists' scissors

◀ *A handful of dried seaweed, a few pieces of coral and some craggy shells are all it takes to compose a seashore decoration for a bathroom or kitchen.*

Seashore

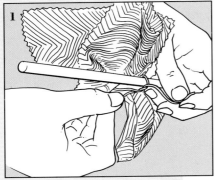

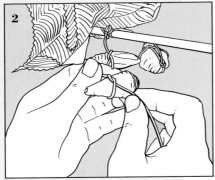

1 Line the inside of the cotton fabric with a double thickness of tissue paper. Place the gift shell in the centre and draw the fabric around it. Knot the leather tightly around the 'neck' of the parcel, then tie it around the cane to secure it diagonally.

2 Tie the leather around one shell after another, leaving a 4-5 cm (1½-2 in) space between them. If necessary, in case the shells start to slip, secure the leather ties with a dab of glue. Glue the starfish to the side of the parcel.

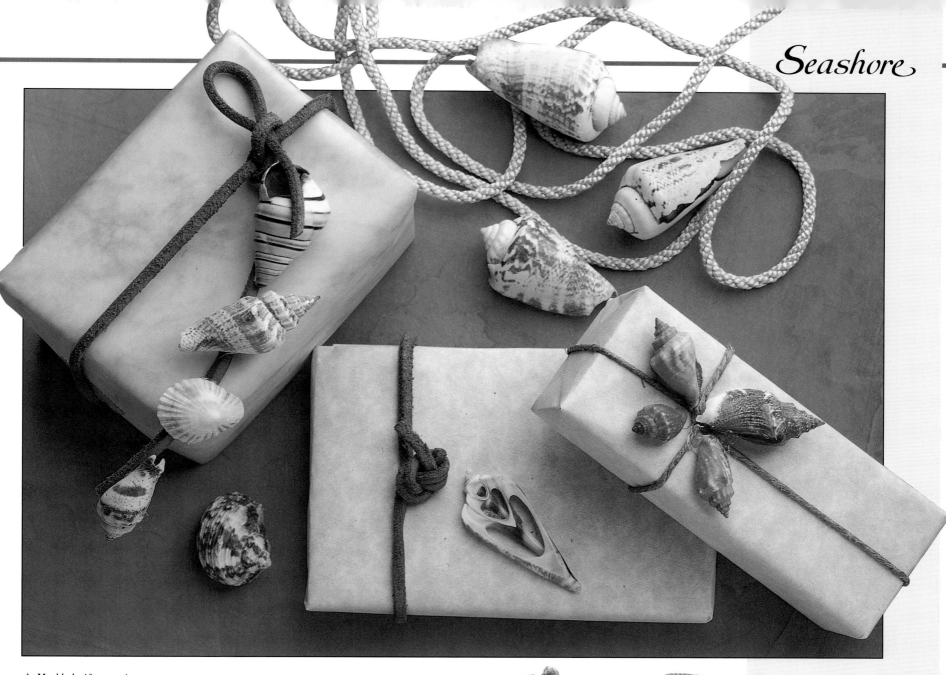

▲ *Marbled gift wrapping papers tied with leather and decorated with clusters, strings and silhouettes of shells.*

◀ *What could be more appropriate to decorate a gift of a beautiful shell? A wavy-striped nautical cotton fabric in red, white and blue is secured with leather thonging and decorated with shells tied around a length of cane.*

You will need:
A piece of cotton fabric
Double thickness of tissue paper
About a 25 cm (10 in) length
of cane
Thin leather thonging
Selection of shells, and a starfish
Hot glue or
clear quick-setting glue

99

You will need:
A basket with straight sides
Clam shells or similar shells
in two sizes
Blue-dyed sea lavender
Dried seaweed
Florists' scissors
Hot glue or
clear quick-setting glue

◀ *A shopping basket of unremarkable appearance takes on a new look when it is covered with light and dark, large and small bivalve shells and filled with an informal grouping of blue sea lavender. It is a pretty decoration for a bathroom.*

▶ *A discarded kitchen jug covered with a wide variety of shells has a look of Victorian opulence, and may itself become a family treasure. You can cover other household items such as bowls, plates and vases in a similar way, using hot glue or clear quick-setting glue.*

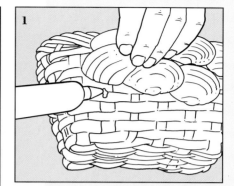

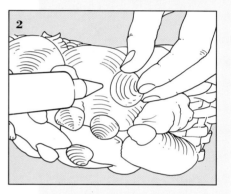

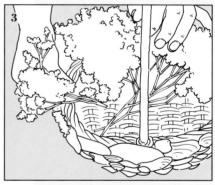

1 *Starting at the top of the basket, stick on a row of larger shells, each one slightly overlapping the next. Continue gluing on the shells until the basket is covered.*

2 *Glue small shells between the rows of the larger ones, adding more to cover any gaps.*

3 *Fill the basket with sprays of sea lavender, criss-crossing the stems to hold them in place. Push short lengths of seaweed between.*

Seashore

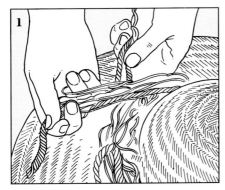

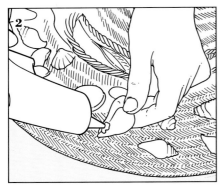

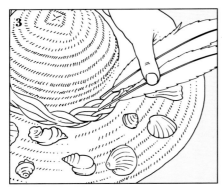

1 *Tie the band around the crown of the hat, leaving the ends to trail.*

2 *Glue the shells in random order around the hat brim, varying the shapes and colours as much as possible.*

3 *Tuck the feathers into the hatband and secure them with a dab of glue.*

◀ *A plain straw hat takes on a jaunty air when it is decorated with a galaxy of seashells and trimmed with a brace of feathers.*

You will need:
A plain straw hat
Rope, braid or cord for hatband
Selection of small shells, as varied as possible
Feathers
Hot glue or clear quick-setting glue

▲ *Comb the beaches for seaweed and seashells and make a stylish two-tone posy to decorate a straw hat. Circle the crown with gold-threaded ribbon to catch the sunlight, and glue on amber-tinged seaweed and shells. This decoration includes turrids, augers, cone shells and Venus clams.*

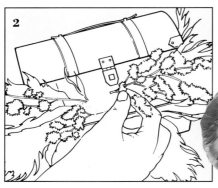

You will need:
A lidded box about
20cm (8 in) wide
Short lengths of dried seaweed
or preserved leaves
Sea lavender, sea holly
and statice
Selection of shells
A plastic prong
Florists' adhesive clay
Dry stem-holding foam
Florists' scissors
Wooden toothpicks
Hot glue or
clear quick-setting glue

1 *Fix the plastic prong to the base of the box with a piece of clay, and press the foam onto it. Arrange short lengths of dried seaweed or preserved leaves to make an elongated shape.*

2 *Insert short lengths of sea lavender and statice to follow the shape and fill in the design.*

▲ *Add a few drops of essential oil to a collection of shells and it becomes a tactile and unusual pot pourri. Put the shells in a lidded container, add two or three drops of oil, stir gently and cover the jar. Leave for a week or so, stirring occasionally, before displaying the now-fragrant shells in small dishes or scallop shells.*

   Select a fragrance from the many oils used to make floral pot pourris, from the sweet scent of rose or lavender oils, through the heady scents of sandalwood or cloves to the refreshing aromas of lemon grass or eucalyptus oils.

▶ *A small oak coffer filled with dry stem-holding foam and spilling over with sea holly and sea lavender, seashells and seaweed makes a long-lasting display that would look good on a hall table or sideboard.*

3 *Position the round, ball-like heads of sea holly evenly throughout the design, with some extending above the box lid.*

4 *Glue the shells to the wooden toothpicks and press them into the foam, arranging some so that they are angled low over the front of the container.*

Seashore

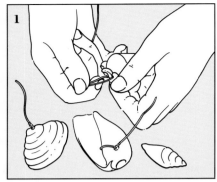

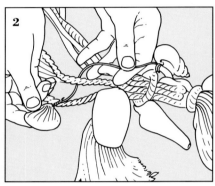

You will need:
Selection of shells
Thick cord with 2 tassels
Silver roll wire
Scissors

1 *If possible, select shells which have a tiny hole in them. Thread a length of fine silver wire through the hole and twist the ends together to secure them. If the shells have no holes, wrap the wire tightly around them and twist the ends. Craggy species such as mitre and nutmeg shells are easiest to wire in this way.*

2 *Test the cord against the curtain to see where the shells will have most impact, then twist the wires tightly around the cord and tassels.*

◀ Shells have just what it takes - subtle colours, fascinating shapes and a variety of textures - to dress up a plain curtain tie-back.

▶ A plain earthenware jug filled to the brim with shells has a collar of frayed rope decorated with conches and nutmeg shells, turrids and cone shells, all simply glued to the rope.

Managing Editor: Jo Finnis
Editor: Geraldine Christy
Design: Nigel Duffield
Photography: Nelson Hargreaves
Illustrations: Geoff Denney Associates
Production: Ruth Arthur, Sally Connolly, Neil Randles,
Karen Staff, Jonathan Tickner
Director of Production: Gerald Hughes